QUIZ FOR ALL

GENERAL PRESS

GENERAL PRESS
4228/1, Second Floor
Ansari Road, Daryaganj
New Delhi - 110002

Ph. : 9911359970, 23282971
e-mail : generalpressindia@gmail.com

First Edition : 2005
Fourth Edition : 2017

ISBN : 9788190276603

Published by Azeem Ahmad Khan for General Press
Printed by Repro Knowledgecast Limited, Thane

Quiz For All

Editors
Azeem Ahmad Khan
Dr. Ruth Premi

Assistant Editors
Sanjay Raghav
Indrani Dutta
Arvind Shrivastava

Art Director
Sydney Mark

Illustrators
Sanjay Verma
Gurdeep Singh

CONTENTS

ANIMALS

1. Which is the fastest land animal?
2. Which is the largest land animal?
3. Which is the largest animal on earth?
4. Which is the tallest land animal?
5. Which is the largest bird in the world?
6. Which is the smallest bird in the world?
7. Name one mammal which can fly.
8. What is the national bird of New Zealand?
9. What is the symbol of WWF?
10. Which is the largest snake in the world?
11. Which is the longest snake in the world?
12. Which is the largest member of the cat family?
13. What is an elephant's tusk made of?
14. What is a baby kangaroo called?
15. What do oysters make?
16. Which bird is used as a symbol of love and peace?
17. Which is the most venomous land snake in the world?
18. Where do the penguins live?
19. Which is the fastest creature on two legs?
20. Which wildlife sanctuary in India is home to the Asiatic lions?

DID YOU KNOW?

- The electric eel can produce powerful electric shocks of up to 500 volts, enough to kill an adult human.
- The reticulated python, found in southeast Asia, is the longest snake in the world, measuring up to 10 m in length.

ANIMALS

21. Which is the largest fish in the world?
22. What do monkeys have that apes do not?
23. What is the long winter sleep in some animals called?
24. Which mammal has the longest gestation period?
25. Which is the largest lizard in the world?
26. Name any three birds that cannot fly.
27. How many legs does a spider have?
28. Where is the Sunderban Tiger Reserve?
29. Which national park in India is the sole habitat of one-horned rhino?
30. Which is the largest bird sanctuary in India?
31. What are the breathing organs of a fish called?
32. What is the colour of a giraffe's tongue?
33. Name a sea animal which has eight arms.
34. Which bird can fly backwards?
35. What do bees gather from flowers for making honey?
36. How many eggs a year does the emperor penguin lay?
37. The height of which animal is measured in 'hands'?
38. Which is the largest reptile in the world?
39. Identify this animal:
40. Which animal sheds its tail when attacked or threatened?

DID YOU KNOW?

- Whale shark, the world's largest fish, can grow up to 12 m in length and weigh up to 20 tonnes.
- The Komodo dragon is the largest lizard in the world, found on some Indonesian islands. Males average 2.25 m in length and weigh about 60 kg.

ANIMALS

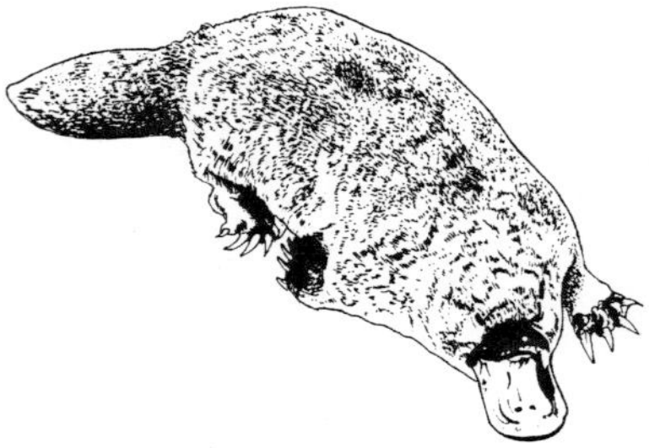

41. Which is the world's largest venomous snake?
42. Name one mammal which lays eggs.
43. Which is the only country where the giant pandas are found?
44. Which is the fastest swimming fish in the world?
45. Which bird lays the biggest egg in the world?
46. What is the study of birds called?
47. Identify this bird:

48. Where is the Gir National Park?
49. What are bird's feathers made of?
50. Which is the fastest flying bird in the world?
51. Which of the big cats have tear stain facial markings?
52. Of what shapes are the cells in bee-hives?
53. What is the national bird of USA?

54. Which animal is also called the 'river horse'?
55. What does the giant panda eat?
56. In a colony of bees, what are male bees called?
57. What is a male horse called?
58. Which bird has the longest bill?

59. Where does a kingfisher make its nest?
60. Which wild animal is the Rann of Kutch famous for?

DID YOU KNOW?

- The blackbuck, a species of deer found in India, can reach speeds of 96 km/h over short distances.
- The king cobra is the largest and longest venomous snake in the world. It measures up to 4.5 m in length and is found in southeast Asia and India.

ANIMALS

61. Which bird travels the most on its migratory journey?
62. Which is the largest carnivorous land animal?
63. Which flat-tailed water animal makes a dam and lives in a lodge?
64. Which is the fastest flying insect?
65. Which desert snake makes a noise with its tail?
66. What is a male deer called?
67. Which is the world's largest eagle?
68. Where does a butterfly have its sense of touch?
69. In which country do you find a koala?
70. Which animal has the longest tongue?
71. Which bird has the largest wingspan?
72. Which animal lays the largest egg?
73. Which is the tallest flying bird?
74. Do the flying squirrels really fly or just glide?
75. What is a flying fox?
76. Where is the Kaziranga National Park?
77. Where do you find the vampire bats?
78. Which is the largest tree-living mammal?
79. In which country do you find the Great Barrier Reef?
80. Which is the only species of parrot that cannot fly?

DID YOU KNOW?

- The peregrine falcon dives at an amazing speed of 360 km/h on its prey, usually small birds, in the air.
- The Arctic tern travels the longest distance during its migratory journey. It covers a round trip of about 36,000 km from the Arctic to the Antarctic and back each year.

ANIMALS

81. What kind of fish is a hammerhead?

82. Which is the slowest mammal on earth?
83. Which mammal is known not to drink water?
84. Which is the most poisonous lizard?
85. What term is used for extracting the poison of a snake?
86. 'Plumage' is the scientific term for which parts of a bird?
87. Which is the shortest snake in the world?

88. Which is the largest member of the deer family?
89. How much does a bee hummingbird, the world's smallest bird, weigh?
90. Where is the Kanha National Park?
91. Which bird lays the largest egg in proportion to its size?

92. Name the bird which is trained by the Chinese to catch fish?
93. Which is the largest bird of prey in the world?
94. Which is the heaviest flying bird?
95. Which country has almost all the 'marsupials' in the world?
96. Mainly which creatures belong to the order *Arachnida*?
97. Which is the largest rodent in the world?

98. Which was the most fierce carnivorous dinosaur?
99. What is the study of insects called?
100. What is the study of animal behaviour called?

DID YOU KNOW?

- The kiwi lays an egg a quarter of her own size. The egg weighs 420 g—the kiwi weighs 1.7 kg.
- Whales are not fish. They are mammals, as they give birth to babies and feed them on milk. They do not have gills like fish and therefore come to the surface every 5–10 minutes to breathe.

PLANTS & TREES

1. Which is the world's biggest flower?
2. Where did the art of bonsai originate?
3. Which substance is responsible for the green colour of leaves?

4. What is grown in paddy fields?
5. What is grown in vineyards?
6. The branch of which tree is used as a symbol of peace?
7. Which is the most widely cultivated fruit in India?
8. Which is the most widely cultivated fruit in the world?
9. Name one fungus which we eat as a vegetable.
10. If tea is made from leaves, what is coffee made from?

11. How is aubergine better known in India?
12. Which is the fastest growing plant?
13. Which is the smelliest flower on earth?
14. What is another name for the hibiscus flower?
15. Which is the single largest mangrove area in the world?
16. What kind of trees are the largest on earth?
17. Which is the only family of fruits that does not rippen after plucking?
18. Which is the world's biggest rainforest?
19. Which is the most poisonous fungus?

20. Which valuable drug is obtained from the bark of cinchona tree?

DID YOU KNOW?

- Some species of the bamboo plant can grow at up to 91 cm (35 inches) per day—fastest of any plant.
- The 'corpse flower' is the smelliest flower on earth. When it blooms, it releases a foul odour similar to that of rotten flesh that can be smelled half a mile away.

The Human Body

1. Which is the largest organ in our body?
2. How many bones are there in the human skeleton?
3. How many times per minute does the human heart beat normally?
4. Deficiency of which vitamin causes night blindness?
5. What is the normal temperature of our body?
6. Which organ is known as the 'sense of touch'?
7. Which is the most common infectious disease?
8. What are the four blood groups?
9. Which substance in the blood is responsible for carrying oxygen to the tissues?
10. How many teeth are known as milk teeth in human beings?
11. How much quantity is there in one unit of blood?
12. What is the soft and fatty substance inside a bone called?
13. Which disease is caused by the deficiency of iodine?
14. Which bones protect the heart and the lungs?
15. Which disease is caused by the bite of a mad dog?
16. What is the medical rating of perfect vision?
17. Which is considered the oldest disease?
18. Which component of blood protects our body from infections?
19. Deficiency of which vitamin causes scurvy?
20. How much blood does an average man have?

DID YOU KNOW?

- Each day our heart beats over 1,00,000 times.
- Colour blindness is the inability to distinguish one or more of the three colours—red, green and blue.

21. Which vitamin helps in blood clotting?
22. Which is the smallest bone in our body?
23. Which is the largest and longest bone in our body?
24. What is the 'Universal Donar' blood group?
25. What is the 'Universal Receiver' blood group?
26. Which part of our body is affected by malaria?
27. What is a doctor who treats our skin and its diseases called?
28. Which is the second largest organ in our body?
29. Which disease is caused by the deficiency of vitamin D?
30. Which element in human diet is considered as a major cause of heart attack?
31. Which disease affects the immune system of our body?
32. What is a doctor who treats illness and disorders of the mind called?
33. Which disease is caused by the imbalance of sugar?
34. Against which disease is the BCG vaccine given?
35. Which part of the body is affected by drinking alcohol?
36. What does the symbol R_x at the beginning of a prescription mean?
37. Which part of our body is affected by tetanus?
38. What is the average weight of an adult human brain?
39. How many bones are there in the human skull?
40. In which part of the human body are red blood cells made?

DID YOU KNOW?

- The coronary heart disease is the most common cause of sudden death.
- Our body contains around 30 billion red blood cells. They are produced in bone marrow, and their function is to carry oxygen and carbon dioxide around the body.

The Human Body

41. What is the medical term for 'loss of memory'?
42. Which part of our eyes is responsible for the colour of the eyes?
43. What is the method of treating an illness by sticking needles into a patient's body known as?
44. Which part of our body is affected by tuberculosis?
45. Name the pigment which is responsible for different skin colours.
46. Which part of the brain deals with our thoughts, emotions and personality?
47. Which gland in our body secretes insulin?
48. Which gland in our body secretes bile juice?
49. What is a doctor who treats heart ailments called?
50. Which gland in our body accumulates iodine?
51. Which part of our body is affected by typhoid?
52. Where are the bones known as the hammer, anvil and stirrup found in our body?
53. Which part of our body is affected by xerophthalmia?
54. What is the main function of insulin in our body?
55. In which condition is dialysis needed?

DID YOU KNOW?

- Each side of the brain controls the opposite side of the body.
- Gul Mohammad of India was the shortest man in the world. When measured in 1990, he was found just 57 cm (22.5 inches) tall.

GENERAL SCIENCE

1. What is the name of our galaxy?
2. Which planet is famous for the rings around it?
3. What is the mouth of a volcano called?
4. How many colours are there in a rainbow?
5. Which is the closest star to the earth?
6. What does CNG stand for?
7. How much time does light take to reach the earth from the sun?

8. Who invented the electric bulb?
9. Which is the hardest known substance in the world?
10. What colour does the earth appear from the space?

11. Does water expand or contract when it freezes?
12. Which is the largest planet in our Solar System?
13. Who was the first man in the world to go into the space?
14. Which instrument is used by doctors for examining the movements of heart and lungs?
15. What was the name of the world's first artificial satellite?

16. Which mineral is used for making match heads?
17. What is inside a thermometer that shines like silver?
18. Who was the first man in the world to land on the moon?
19. Which causes a more severe burn—boiling water or steam?
20. What is used for coating in nonstick frying pans?

DID YOU KNOW?

- The air contains 78% nitrogen, 21% oxygen and 1% carbon dioxide and other gases.
- Astronauts become a little taller in space. Because there is less gravity, so their bones are less squashed together.

GENERAL SCIENCE

21. Which is the lightest gas?

22. Which travels faster—light or sound?
23. Which is the commonest phobia in the world?
24. Which virus causes AIDS?
25. What is the thin wire in an electric bulb that glows called?
26. Which gas is added to drinks to make them fizzy?
27. Which gas protects the earth from the harmful ultraviolet rays of the sun?
28. Who invented the lift?
29. What is used for detecting the direction and range of an approaching aircraft?
30. What is the chemical name of table salt?
31. What is the other name for 'leukemia'?
32. At what temperature does water freeze?
33. At what temperature does water boil?
34. What is the full form of AIDS?
35. What is the path of a planet or satellite called?
36. Who propounded 'The Theory of Evolution'?
37. What is the chief constitute of gobar gas?
38. Which gas in automobile exhaust can cause cancer?
39. What does a Light Year measure?
40. Which instrument is used for measuring the distance travelled by a vehicle?

DID YOU KNOW?

- It is possible to see the planets Mercury, Venus, Mars, Jupiter and Saturn with naked eye.
- PARAM 10000, developed in 1998, is India's most powerful indigenous supercomputer and Asia's second-most powerful supercomputer. It is capable of 100 billion calculations per second.

General Science

41. Who was the first Indian woman to go into the space?
42. How many carats are there in pure gold?
43. Who invented the dynamite?
44. What is the chemical name for chalk?
45. Who wrote 'The Origin of Species'?
46. Which gas is responsible for the Green House Effect?
47. What can travel faster than light?
48. What colour does the sky appear from the moon?
49. In which country did homeopathy originate?

50. Who was the first scientist to propose that the sun is the centre of our Solar System?
51. What unit is used to measure the speed of a ship?
52. Who invented the printing press?
53. Neil Armstrong was the first man to step on the moon. Who followed him a few minutes later?
54. Which bomb was created in the Manhattan Project?
55. Who was the first mathematician to introduce zero to the world?
56. Which is the most abundant element in the universe?
57. Which metal is often used for making electrical wires and contacts?
58. Which is a better reflector of light—a black surface or a white surface?
59. Which electrical instrument is used for increasing or reducing the voltage?
60. Which instrument is used in submarines to observe the objects above the sea level?

DID YOU KNOW?

- The fastest speed possible in the universe is the speed of light—around 3,00,000 km/s. This means that when you look at the moon, you see it as it was about 1.3 seconds ago, and the sun around 8.3 minutes ago.

General Science

61. What is the basic material used in computer chips?
62. Who discovered the lightning conductor?
63. Who invented the dynamo?
64. Which acid is used in car batteries?
65. Why do fighter planes fly at great heights?
66. Which gas is generally used in illuminated signboards?
67. Which instrument is used for recording the movements of the heart?
68. In which year did Neil Armstrong and Edwin Aldrin land on the moon?
69. What is the unit of electrical power?
70. Who discovered that plants have life?

71. Where is India's rocket launching station situated?
72. Which US scientist has ever obtained the most patents to his credit?
73. Which is the fifth largest planet in our Solar System?
74. Who invented the pneumatic bicycle tyre?
75. What is the full form of ISRO?
76. What is the full form of NASA?
77. What device in a car engine mixes air with petrol vapour for combustion?
78. What unit is used to express the power of spectacles?
79. What is the name of the biggest telescope installed in the space by the European Space Agency and NASA?
80. What is the flight data recorder carried by almost all modern aircraft called?

DID YOU KNOW?

- The deepest hole ever drilled into the earth's crust is 12.26 km deep.
- Thomas Alva Edison holds the world record for the most patents held by a single person with 1,093, either on his own or jointly.

General Science

81. How is an astronaut better known in Russia?
82. What is the centre of a hurricane called?
83. Which planet looks red?
84. Which is the most abundant element in the earth's atmosphere?
85. What is the voltage of a dry cell in a torch battery?
86. Which element is known as quicksilver?
87. Which instrument is used for measuring the magnitude of an earthquake?
88. Who said, "A small step for man—a giant leap for mankind"?
89. What does GPS stand for?
90. What is the shape of the earth's orbit around the sun?
91. Which Italian astronomer discovered the rings of Saturn?
92. Which is the better conductor of sound—air or wood?
93. What is added to the dough of bread to make it rise?

94. What is the subject of the book, 'Charaka Samhita'?
95. What is the branch of science which deals with the study of light called?
96. What did Benjamin Franklin use to discover the electricity in lightning?
97. Which instrument is used for measuring the velocity and force of wind?
98. What was the name of the spacecraft that carried Neil Armstrong to the moon?
99. Which two radioactive elements were discovered by Marie Curie and Pierre Curie?
100. Who was the first Indian to propose that the earth is spherical and rotates on its own axis?

DID YOU KNOW?

- The light and energy of the sun come from nuclear reactions deep inside the sun itself.
- The noise of thunder is caused by the rapid expansion of the air which the lightning has heated to more than 33,000°C.

GENERAL SCIENCE

101. Which are the only two planets, which do not have any satellites?

102. Which element is generally used in the electric bulb filaments?

103. Who discovered the vaccination?

104. Who discovered the penicillin?

105. Who discovered 'The Theory of Relativity'?

106. What is a shooting star?

107. What is the unit of sound?

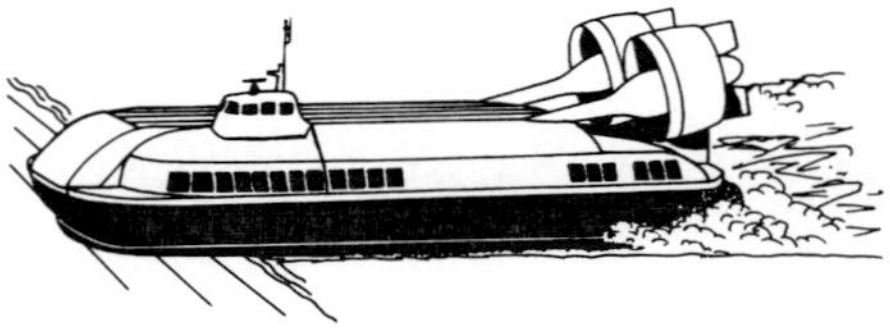

108. Who invented the helicopter?

109. Who invented the hovercraft?

110. When was Yuri Gagarin went into the space?

111. Who is known as 'The Father of Indian Nuclear Science'?

112. Which instrument is used to receive and transmit signals in a satellite?

113. Which star appears to be the brightest to the naked human eye?

114. Which Indian mathematician invented algebra?

115. What term is used for the rapid spread of a disease among many people in the same place?

116. Which acid is found in milk?

117. Which is the nearest star to the earth after the sun?

118. Who discovered the principle of electromagnetic induction?

119. What name is given to the reflected sound waves in a cave or an empty hall?

120. Which branch of science deals with the study of the relationship between living organisms and their environment?

DID YOU KNOW?

- ❖ The planet Neptune has the fastest winds in our Solar System. They blow at around 2,400 km/h.
- ❖ The fastest wind speed recorded on earth is 486 km/h, associated with a large tornado in Oklahoma, USA, on May 3, 1999.

GENERAL SCIENCE

121. Name one metal which is liquid at room temperature.

122. Where is the Sea of Tranquillity?

123. Who discovered the blood circulation?

124. What is a doctor who treats animal diseases and injuries called?

125. What is the speed of sound in air?

126. What is the speed of light in air?

127. What important compound was found on the moon in 1998?

128. Which alloy contains the metals copper and zinc?

129. What is the scientific name of laughing gas?

130. Which two acids are found in the acid rain?

131. Which branch of science deals with the forecasting of weather?

132. Name the gases that make up most stars.

133. What does a sphygmomanometer measure?

134. Which metal is most abundantly found in the earth's crust?

135. By what name is acetylsalicylic acid better known?

136. What term denotes the time taken for the Solar System to revolve once around the Milky Way?

137. Which Indian won the Nobel Prize for Medicine in 1968?

138. Who propounded the quantum theory?

139. What does a sudden fall in the barometer reading indicate?

140. Where is America's spaceship launching station situated?

DID YOU KNOW?

- The temperature of the flame from a gas burner is about 2,000°C.
- Scientists have discovered supermassive black holes which reside in the hearts of galaxies and can be as massive as several hundred million times that of the sun.

SPORTS

1. How many rings are there in the Olympic flag?
2. Which game is Baichung Bhutia associated with?
3. Which is the biggest sports festival in the world?
4. How many squares are there in a chess board?
5. How many players are there in a team of basketball?
6. In which year did India win the World Cup in cricket?

7. What is a 'duck' in cricket?
8. What is the national game of USA?
9. Which country has won the most Gold Medals in the Olympic hockey?
10. What is the colour of the highest belt in karate?
11. What is the length of a cricket pitch?
12. What is the width of a football goal?
13. At what height are the baskets hung in basketball?
14. Where is the Wankhede Stadium?
15. What is the meaning of 'karate'?

16. What is the playground of wrestling called?
17. Who is popularly known as 'Black Pearl'?
18. How many pieces, excluding the striker, are there on the board when a carrom game starts?
19. Which is the largest indoor stadium in India?
20. Which country has won the most World Cup Soccer Tournaments?

DID YOU KNOW?

- Brazil has won the World Cup Soccer Tournament five times—in 1958, 1962, 1970, 1994 and 2002.
- Major Rajyavardhan Singh Rathore has won a Silver Medal in double trap shooting at the 2004 Athens Olympics.

Sports

21. Where were the Olympic Games originated?
22. Which ball game is played in the largest ground?

23. What is the national game of Russia?
24. Which game is Mike Tyson associated with?
25. Which game is also known as ping-pong?
26. Who was the captain of the Indian cricket team that won the World Cup in 1983?
27. Which is the highest sports award given to sportspersons in India?
28. Which country has won the most World Cup Cricket Tournaments?
29. What is the traditional wrestling of Japan called?

30. In whose honour was August 29 chosen as the National Sports Day in India?
31. What colour ring in the Olympic flag represents Asia?
32. Which is the only game to allow only right-handed players?
33. Who is the only woman tennis player to win the Wimbledon singles title nine times?
34. Which sporting activity makes the most use of all the body muscles?
35. Which game the Ambedkar Stadium is associated with?

36. Which country always leads the March Past during the opening ceremony in the Olympics?
37. Who is the first Indian Chess Grandmaster?
38. Who was the world's youngest cricket captain?
39. Which is the highest sports award given to sports coaches in India?
40. The wood of which tree is generally used for making the cricket bats?

DID YOU KNOW?

- Australia has won the World Cup Cricket Tournament three times—in 1987, 1999 and 2003.
- Martina Navratilova of USA has won nine Wimbledon women's singles titles.

SPORTS

41. Which is the oldest football tournament in India?
42. What is the duration of a normal hockey match?
43. Who was the first Indian woman to reach the finals of an Olympic athletic event?
44. Which game the Davis Cup is associated with?
45. Where did the game of polo originate?
46. Which was the first computer to defeat a Grandmaster in chess?
47. Which cricket stadium in India has the largest seating capacity?
48. Which game is Karnam Malleswari associated with?
49. Which country hosted the first World Cup Soccer Tournament?
50. What is a ball used in ice-hockey called?
51. Which is considered the fastest team game in the world?

52. In which year did the Olympic Games revive in Athens?
53. Which Indian holds the world record of scoring the highest number of runs in One-Day International cricket matches?
54. Which game is Ronaldo associated with?
55. What is the full form of FIFA?
56. In which game are more balls used—billiards or snooker?
57. Who holds the world record of scoring the highest number of runs in a Test innings?
58. Which is the only country to have played in every World Cup Soccer Tournament?
59. Who is the youngest heavyweight boxing champion of the world?
60. Where were the first modern Olympic Games held?

DID YOU KNOW?

- Prakash Padukone has won nine successive Golds in national tournaments from 1971–79.
- The Durand Cup, first played at Shimla in 1888, is the oldest football tournament in India and the third oldest in the world.

SPORTS

61. What is the national game of Spain?
62. In which tournament is the Golden Boot Award given?
63. Which game is Sania Mirza associated with?
64. Which cricket player finished his test match career with a batting average of 99.94?

65. What was the original name of Muhammad Ali?
66. Where is the Dhyan Chand Stadium in India?
67. Who was the first Indian to win a Grand Slam title in tennis?
68. Who is the only man to win the 100 m sprint twice at the Olympics?
69. Which Asian country has won the World Cup Soccer Tournament?
70. Which Indian player has won the national title for badminton nine times in a row?
71. How many days do the Summer Olympic Games last?
72. Who won a Bronze Medal for India in weightlifting in Sydney Olympics, 2000?
73. Who won a Silver Medal for India in double trap shooting in Athens Olympics, 2004?
74. How many goals in all have been scored by Dhyan Chand in the Olympics?
75. Which is the largest stadium in the world in terms of seating capacity?
76. Which game the Irani Trophy is associated with?
77. Which Indian cricketer is called the 'Tiger'?
78. Where was Major Dhyan Chand born?
79. Who was the first Indian lady Grandmaster?
80. Which Pakistani cricketer has played in six World Cup Cricket Tournaments?

DID YOU KNOW?

- ❖ The highest score in One-Day Internationals is 398 by Sri Lanka against Kenya in 1996.
- ❖ The highest score of India in One-Day Internationals is 376 against New Zealand (1999) and the lowest score is 54 against Sri Lanka (2000).

SPORTS

81. Which country will host the 2006 World Cup Soccer Tournament?

82. Which game the William Cup is associated with?

83. Who is said to be 'The Father of Modern Olympics'?

84. Which game the Thomas Cup is associated with?

85. Which world renowned sportsman is associated with the slogan, "I am the greatest"?

86. Who was the first Indian bowler to take a hat-trick in a One-Day International cricket match?

87. What distance has to be covered in a modern marathon?

88. Which country did not win the World Cup Cricket Tournament even once, although it has reached the finals on three occasions?

89. Which Indian batsman made three consecutive centuries in his first three Test matches?

90. Which American track-and-field athlete won nine Olympic Golds in the 1980s and 1990s?

91. When did women first participate in the Olympics?

92. The poles used by the pole-vaulters in international meets are made of what?

93. In which year was the FIFA founded in Paris?

94. Which boxer gained the international attention as the light heavyweight champion in the Rome Olympics, 1960?

95. Where are the headquarters of the International Olympic Committee?

DID YOU KNOW?

- Pete Sampras of USA has won seven Wimbledon men's singles titles.
- The Maracana Municipal Stadium in Rio de Janeiro, Brazil, is the world's largest football stadium, with a normal capacity for 2,05,000 spectators.

HISTORY

1. Who was the founder of Mughal Empire in India?
2. Who was the supreme leader of Germany in World War II?
3. Who were the first Europeans to trade with India?
4. In which Indian city did the revolt of 1857 begin?
5. Who gave the Kohinoor diamond its name?
6. Who was the Rajput princess whom Akbar married?

7. In which year did India become a Republic?
8. Which Sikh Guru did Jahangir execute?
9. Who was the last ruler of Mughal dynasty?
10. Who was the son and successor of Akbar?
11. Whose daughter was Razia Sultana?
12. When were the first General Elections held in India?
13. Where was the first session of Indian National Congress held?
14. Who emerged as a great leader after the Russian Revolution?

15. Who was the first European to invade India?
16. Which ancient civilization was the birthplace of democracy?
17. Which British officer ordered his men to fire at innocents in the Jallianwala Bagh massacre?
18. Where did the East India Company set up its first factory in India?
19. Between which two countries was the Tashkant Agreement signed?
20. Which city did Akbar, Jahangir and Shah Jahan use as their capital?

DID YOU KNOW?

- The Egyptians took as much as 70 days to mummify a human body.
- Harappa and Mohenjo-daro, situated in the Indus Valley in modern Pakistan and India, were among the world's very advanced civilizations.

HISTORY

21. Who was the son and successor of Babar?
22. Which Empire was Ashoka associated with?
23. Where did the Jallianwala Bagh massacre take place?
24. In which year was the UNO founded?
25. Where was Napoleon exiled?
26. Who was Shivaji's son and successor?
27. Who built the famous Peacock Throne?
28. What was the Jahangir's earlier name?
29. Which Mughal Emperor was exiled to Burma by the British?
30. From where did Mahatma Gandhi start his historical Dandi March?
31. What name the British Government gave to India's First War of Independence?
32. Name the two companions of Bhagat Singh who were hanged along with him.
33. Who was the Nawab of Bengal when the British Forces won the battle of Plassey?
34. Who was the Mughal Emperor who died of a sudden fall from a staircase?
35. Which king's or queen's reign has been the longest in the English history?
36. Chanakya was advisor to which Emperor?
37. What was the name of Samrat Ashoka's father?
38. When did the partition of Bengal take place?
39. Which incident on December 7, 1941, forced the Americans to enter the World War II?
40. On which plain in northern India have three decisive battles been fought in 1526, 1556 and 1761?

DID YOU KNOW?

- On December 7, 1941, Japanese planes attacked the American naval base at Pearl Harbour, Hawaii and killed over 2,000 naval officers and men. Following this attack, America joined the Allies in the Second World War.

HISTORY

41. Which political party was in power in Britain when India achieved independence?
42. Which Governor-General was associated with the partition of Bengal?
43. Who defeated Napoleon in the battle of Waterloo?
44. In which battle did Babar defeat Ibrahim Lodhi to establish the Mughal Empire in India?

45. What were the Egyptian kings called?
46. Which two countries fought the Hundred Years' War?
47. Who did Alexander defeat in the Battle of Hydaspes?
48. In whose honour did Akbar build the palace-city of Fatehpur Sikri?
49. When was the Indian National Congress founded?
50. Who is credited for the integration of princely states into the Indian Union after independence?

51. Which US President made the decision to drop the atom bombs on Hiroshima and Nagasaki in 1945?
52. Who carried away Shah Jahan's famous Peacock Throne and the Kohinoor diamond to Iran?
53. Which Mughal Emperor was declared the leader of Indian troops during the revolt of 1857?

54. Between whom was the American War of Independence fought?
55. Which international organization was formed after the World War I to preserve the international peace and security?

DID YOU KNOW?

- Aristotle, the Greek philosopher, was the tutor of Alexander the Great.
- The first atom bomb was dropped on Hiroshima on August 6, 1945 and the second was dropped on Nagasaki on August 9, 1945.

GEOGRAPHY

1. Which is the longest river in India?
2. Which is the longest river in the world?
3. Which is the largest river in the world?
4. Which is Asia's longest river?
5. Which is the largest desert in India?
6. Which is the largest desert in Asia?
7. Which is the largest desert in the world?
8. Which is the highest waterfall in India?
9. Which is the highest waterfall in the world?
10. Which is the largest delta in the world?
11. Which is the highest mountain peak in the world?
12. Which is the highest mountain peak in Indian territory?
13. Which is the largest and deepest Ocean?
14. Which is the largest freshwater lake in the world?
15. Which is the largest saltwater lake in the world?
16. What percentage of the earth's surface area does water occupy?
17. Which continent does not have any desert?
18. Which place in India receives the maximum amount of rainfall annually?
19. Which is the lowest point on the earth?
20. Which is the largest sea in the world?

DID YOU KNOW?

- The Atlantic Ocean is getting wider, but the Pacific Ocean is shrinking.
- Over 250 million years ago all of today's continents were joined together as one supercontinent, named 'Pangea'.

GEOGRAPHY

21. Which is the smallest state in India?
22. Which is the largest state in India?
23. Which city is called 'The Gateway of India'?
24. Where is the Science City in India?
25. Which city is the capital of two Indian states?
26. Which Indian state has two capitals?
27. What is the capital of Uttaranchal?
28. After how many years does the 'census' take place in India?
29. How many states and union territories are there in India?
30. What is the city of Jamshedpur also called?
31. Where is the Marina Beach in India?
32. How is Banaras better known today?
33. Which is the most populous state in India?
34. Which is the least populous state in India?
35. Which Indian city has the highest population density?
36. Which country has the longest international boundary with India?
37. Who founded the city of Fatehpur Sikri?
38. What is the meaning of 'Himalaya'?
39. Which is the largest city of Uttar Pradesh?
40. Which is the largest saltwater lake in India?

DID YOU KNOW?

- The total surface area of the earth is about 51,00,65,000 sq. km.
- According to scientists, a mass of rock must be at least 500 m high in order to be considered a mountain. Anything smaller than that is just a hill.

GEOGRAPHY

41. Which is the largest country in the world?
42. Which is the smallest country in the world?
43. What was the earlier name of Japan?
44. What is the height of Mount Everest?
45. Which continent is known as 'The Dark Continent'?
46. Which is the most populous country in the world?
47. Which is the saltiest sea in the world?
48. What is the capital of Australia?
49. Who discovered America?
50. Which country is known as 'The Gift of the Nile'?
51. What was the earlier name of the Netherlands?
52. What name is given to the original natives of North America?
53. Which country is known as 'The Land of Thunderbolt'?
54. What is the meaning of 'Eskimo'?
55. Which capital city is situated on the banks of the river Thames?
56. Which country has the most number of earthquakes?
57. Which is the wettest place in the world?
58. Which is the driest place on earth?
59. Which is the largest city in the United States?
60. Who was the first man to sail round the world?

DID YOU KNOW?

- Between 1950 and 1990, the world's population has doubled from about 2.5 billion to 5 billion.
- Mawsynram in Meghalaya, with an annual average rainfall of 467 inches, is the wettest place in the world, closely followed by Cherrapunji with 450 inches.

GEOGRAPHY

61. Which Indian state has the longest coastline?
62. Which is the deepest point in the oceans?
63. What is a person who draws maps and charts called?
64. Which country is known as 'The Playground of Europe'?
65. Where is Darjeeling in India?
66. What is another name of United Kingdom?
67. On the banks of which river is Kolkata situated?
68. What is the capital of Israel?
69. Which is the only cold desert in India?
70. Which state in India has borders with the largest number of other states?
71. Name an African country which has all five vowels in its name.
72. Which is the longest beach in India?
73. In which continent is the Sahara desert?
74. Does a north wind blow from the North or to the North?
75. Which river carries the most water in the world?
76. How is Persia better known today?
77. Name the Indian states which are often referred to as 'The Seven Sisters'?
78. Name the country which has an entire continent for itself.
79. Which city stands at the confluence of the Ganga, Yamuna and Saraswati?
80. How is Patliputra better known today?

DID YOU KNOW?

- Tokyo is the world's most populous city, with an estimated population of 2.65 crores.
- The Amazon river of South America discharges water into the Atlantic Ocean at an average of 2,00,000 m^3/sec, increasing to more than 3,40,000 m^3/sec in full flood.

GEOGRAPHY

81. Which is the most populous city in the world?
82. Which city is known as 'The Roof of the World'?
83. What is the breakaway part of a glacier called?
84. How is Peking better known today?
85. Which is the most populous state of USA?
86. On the banks of which river, Srinagar is situated?
87. Which is the largest island in the world?
88. Which state is the largest producer of diamonds in India?
89. Which continent does Brazil belong to?
90. Which Indian city was founded by Maharaja Sawai Jai Singh in 1727?
91. What are the natives of the Netherlands called?
92. Which Indian state's name means 'The Abode of God'?
93. In which Indian state is the Wular Lake located?
94. What are the treeless plains of polar regions called?
95. What is the capital of Greece?
96. Which country leads the world in the production of gold?
97. Which four countries together form the Great Britain?
98. Where is the world's highest waterfall, the Angel Falls?
99. Who discovered the sea-route from Europe to India via the Cape of Good Hope?
100. Which is the longest canal in India?

DID YOU KNOW?

- Hot deserts cover about 20% of the earth's land surface.
- The country that receives the most legal immigrants is the USA. It received 6,31,40,227 official immigrants between 1820 and 1996.

GEOGRAPHY

101. Which country has the longest coastline?
102. Which is the deepest lake in the world?
103. What is Johannesburg famous for?
104. What is known as 'The Sorrow of Bengal'?
105. Which is the largest city in China?
106. Which two countries share the world's longest boundary?
107. Which capital city is situated on the banks of the river Seine?
108. Which Indian state is surrounded on three sides by Bangladesh?
109. Which is the longest canal in the world?
110. What is the boundary line between India and China called?
111. In which country do you find the Suez Canal?
112. Where is the Silicon Valley in the USA?
113. Which is the second highest mountain peak in the world?
114. How many states are there in the USA?
115. Where is the Hudson Bay?
116. Which is the world's longest glacier?
117. What is a small lake located in an abandoned meander loop of a river channel called?
118. On which river is the Bhakra Nangal Dam, the highest dam in India, situated?
119. Which Indian city is known as 'The Queen of the Arabian Sea'?
120. Which canal connects the Red Sea and the Mediterranean Sea?

DID YOU KNOW?

- The Lake Baikal in Siberia, Russia, is the world's largest freshwater lake by volume. With an estimated volume of 23,000 km^3, it contains one-fifth of all the world's fresh surface water. It is also the world's deepest lake with a maximum depth of 1,637 m.

GEOGRAPHY

121. Which is the largest state in the USA?

122. On which river is Aswan Dam built?

123. Which is the highest freshwater lake in the world?

124. Christmas Island is a territory of which country?

125. Which is the world's largest gorge?

126. Which Indian city did Vasco da Gama first visit?

127. On which river do you find the Victoria Falls?

128. Which country is known as 'The Holy Land'?

129. On the banks of which river, Rome is situated?

130. Which is the largest man-made canal in the world?

131. Which river is known as 'The Sorrow of China'?

132. Which Indian hill station's name means 'Place of the Thunderbolt'?

133. Which city founded by Akbar in 1583means 'The City of God'?

134. In which country is the source of Amazon river?

135. How is Gold Coast better known today?

136. Which part of India was liberated from the Portuguese rule in 1961?

137. Which river crosses the equator twice?

138. The Raja, Rani, Rocket and Roarer together make up which of the Indian waterfalls?

139. Which two countries are separated by the Palk Strait?

140. Which is the youngest mountain range in the world?

DID YOU KNOW?

❖ Mongolia is the most sparsely populated country, with a population density of 1.6 people per sq. km while Monaco is the most densely populated country. It has a population density of 16,500 people per sq. km.

Geography

141. Which state in India means 'The Land of the Rising Sun'?
142. Who was the first man in the world to reach the South Pole?
143. Where is the Grand Canyon?
144. Which river flows through the Grand Canyon?
145. Where is the 'Death Valley' located?
146. Which is the world's longest mountain range?
147. Which is the largest mountain range in Europe?
148. Which mountains serve as a boundary between Europe and Asia?
149. Where do you find the Niagara Falls?
150. What area was leased in 1898 by the Chinese to the English for 99 years?
151. Which Indian state was previously called the United Provinces?
152. What is the approximate length of India's coastline?
153. Which river forms the Jog Falls, the highest waterfall in India?
154. The rivers Jhelum, Chenab, Ravi, Beas and Sutlej are tributaries of which river?
155. Which is the largest island in the Indian Ocean?
156. Which Indian territory was occupied by the Japanese from 1942–45 during the World War II?
157. Where are the headquarters of the Geographical Survey of India?
158. In which region does the Toda tribe inhabit in India?
159. Which state did the USA buy from Russia in 1867?
160. What kind of rock is formed by the cooling and solidification of magma?

DID YOU KNOW?

- France is the most popular tourist destination in the world.
- The Alps are Europe's largest mountain range—1,000 km long, up to 250 km wide and covering about 2,10,000 sq. km.

Cinema

1. Which Indian film maker received the lifetime Oscar Award in 1991?

2. Who was the first Indian to win an Oscar Award?
3. Who directed the Bollywood blockbuster *Sholay*?
4. Which was the first Indian talkie film?
5. Which was the first talkie film in English?
6. Which was the first Hollywood movie to be dubbed in Hindi?

7. Who directed the movie 'Titanic'?
8. Which country leads the world in the production of films?
9. How is Yousuf Khan better known in Bollywood?
10. Which Indian film superstar made his debut in *Sat Hindustani*?
11. Who played the title role in *Gandhi* in 1982?

12. Which awards are presented every year by the Academy of Motion Picture Arts and Sciences?
13. During the shooting of which film was Amitabh Bachchan seriously injured?
14. Who directed the movie 'Jurassic Park'?
15. Who won the most Oscars in a lifetime?

16. Who directed the movie 'Mother India'?
17. Who is considered 'The Father of Indian Cinema'?
18. Which Indian singer holds the world record for maximum number of song recordings to her credit?
19. Which film has used the most number of 'extras'?
20. Name the Hindi film in which Sanjiv Kumar played nine different roles.

DID YOU KNOW?

- Titanic is the world's most expensive film ever made. It won 11 Oscars from 14 nominations in 1998.
- India produces more feature films than any other country. Between 700–900 films are produced in India in over 15 languages each year.

Famous Personalities

1. Who was the first Indian to receive a Nobel Prize?
2. Who was the first President of India?
3. Who created the famous cartoon character Micky Mouse?
4. Who is regarded as the architect of the Indian Constitution?
5. Who composed our national anthem?

6. Who composed our national song?
7. Who founded the 'Missionaries of Charity'?
8. Whose birthday is celebrated as Teachers' Day in India?
9. Who said, "Genius is 1 per cent inspiration and 99 per cent perspiration"?
10. Who was the youngest Prime Minister of India?

11. Who created the famous comic character *Chacha Chaudhary*?
12. Who was the first Indian woman to climb Mount Everest?
13. Where was Charlie Chaplin born?
14. Who gave the famous slogan, *Inquilab Zindabad*?
15. Who was the first surgeon in the world to perform the successful human heart transplant?

16. Who was the first woman in the world to climb Mount Everest?
17. Who was the first Indian woman to win the Miss World title?
18. Who was the first President of USA?
19. Name the architect who designed New Delhi.
20. Which Indian has the most number of roads named after him?

DID YOU KNOW?

- ❖ Dr. Rajendra Prasad won the presidential election of 1952 by a majority of 99.3%.
- ❖ Leonardo da Vinci (1452–1519) drew his plans for a helicopter hundreds of years before flying machines were actually invented.

FAMOUS PERSONALITIES

21. Who is the first woman in the world to climb Mount Everest twice?

22. Which US President abolished slavery in America?
23. Who wrote the song, *Sare Jahan Se Achcha*?
24. Who was the first woman IPS officer in India?
25. Which country did Sir Edmund Hillary belong to?
26. Who is known as 'The Father of India's Missile Programme'?

27. Which Indian Prime Minister died in Russia?
28. Who founded the Banaras Hindu University?
29. Who was the first Asian to get a Nobel Prize for Literature?
30. Who has served as the acting Prime Minister of India twice?
31. Who gave Gandhiji the title of *Mahatma*?

32. Who gave Rabindranath Tagore the title of *Gurudev*?
33. Who was the first lady Prime Minister of a country?
34. Who is known as 'The Nightingale of India'?
35. Name the musician who was counted among the nine jewels in the court of Akbar.
36. Who was the heroic Prime Minister of Britain during the World War II.

37. Which Indian Prime Minister's *Samadhi* is called 'Vir Bhoomi'?
38. Who was also known as 'Vishnugupta' or 'Kautilya'?
39. Whose death anniversary is observed as Anti-terrorism Day in India?
40. Whose autobiography is 'The Fall of a Sparrow'?

DID YOU KNOW?

- Marie Curie was the first woman to receive the Nobel Prize.
- Sir David Attenborough of UK holds the world record for the longest working career as a writer and presenter of TV nature programmes.

FAMOUS PERSONALITIES

41. Who is known as 'The Lady of the Lamp'?
42. Who is the most honoured Indian ornithologist?
43. Who is considered the founder of Red Cross?
44. Who introduced the rupee into India?
45. Who was the first lady Prime Minister of Pakistan?
46. Who founded the Indian National Congress?

47. Where was Mahatma Gandhi born?
48. Who is the only woman to have received two Nobel Prizes in different disciplines?
49. Which Indian President occupied the office for the shortest term?
50. Who was the first woman judge of Supreme Court of India?
51. Who was the first President of Indian National Congress?

52. Who founded the modern nursing system?
53. Whose *Samadhi* do you find at 'Vijay Ghat'?
54. Who invented a system of reading and writing for the blind?
55. Who was the longest serving Chief Minister in India?
56. Name the cartoonist with whom the series 'You Said It' is associated.

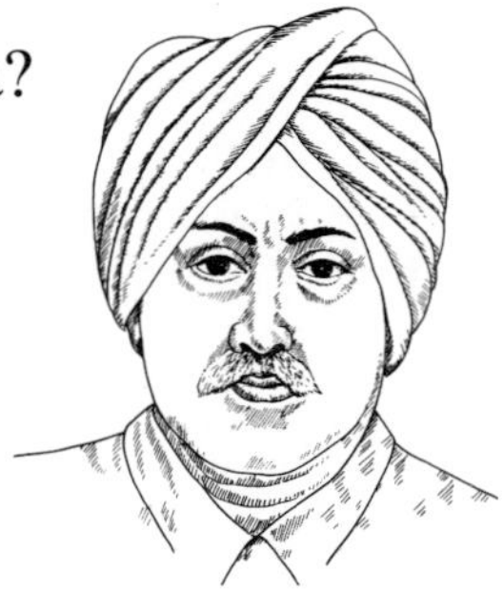

57. Who was the first person to start publishing newspaper in India?
58. What place did Tansen come from?
59. Which prominent Indian freedom fighter died after being injured in a lathi charge at Lahore?
60. Who was popularly known as 'The Tiger of Mysore'?

DID YOU KNOW?

- R.K. Laxman's cartoon feature 'You Said It' has been appearing in The Times of India since 1951.
- Apa Sherpa of Nepal holds the world record of most conquests of Mount Everest. He completed his 13th successful climb of Mount Everest in May 2002.

FAMOUS PERSONALITIES

61. Who was the first lady Prime Minister of Britain?

62. Who designed the city of Chandigarh?
63. Who was the first President of India to be elected unopposed?
64. Who founded the Aligarh Muslim University?
65. Who was popularly known as 'The Frontier Gandhi'?
66. Where was Premchand born?
67. Who founded the 'Brahmo Samaj'?
68. Who is the subject of the book, 'Something Beautiful for God'?

69. Who was the first foreigner to receive the Bharat Ratna?
70. Who was the first Indian surgeon to conduct the successful human heart transplant?
71. After whom was the Mount Everest named?
72. Who is known as the wisest king of the ancient times?
73. Who was the first woman President of Indian National Congress?

74. Who was the first occupant of the Rashtrapati Bhavan?
75. In which country was Adolf Hitler born?
76. Who is the first Asian to win a Nobel Prize for Economics?
77. Who went to England and shot dead General Dyer to avenge the Jallianwala Bagh massacre?
78. The death anniversary of which leader is observed as Martyrs' Day in India?
79. Which Indian astronaut died in the Columbia Space Shuttle explosion in 2003?
80. Who founded the Shantiniketan which is now known as Vishwabharati University?

DID YOU KNOW?

- Yuri Gagarin survived the first manned spaceflight but died in a plane crash seven years later.
- Adolf Hitler's early ambition was to become an art student, but he failed twice to secure entry to the Academy of Fine Arts.

FAMOUS PERSONALITIES

81. Who was the first Indian woman to swim across the English Channel?

82. Who fought to obtain the full civil rights for American Negroes?

83. In which country was Albert Einstein born?

84. Which Indian Prime Minister has never faced the Lok Sabha even once?

85. How is Agnes Gonxha Bojaxhiu better known to the world?

86. Who was the first US President to occupy the White House?

87. Which famous writer and the Nobel Laureate was born in 1865 in Mumbai?

88. Which Governor-General took active interest in the abolition of *Sati Pratha*?

89. Who founded the 'Arya Samaj'?

90. Who was the tutor of Alexander the Great?

91. In which year was William Shakespeare born?

92. Who was popularly known as 'The Fuhrer'?

93. Who invented the shorthand/stenography?

94. Who was the first Indian President of International Court of Justice?

95. Who returned the title of 'Sir' in protest against the Jallianwala Bagh massacre?

96. Who was the first Indian to become the member of British Parliament?

97. Who was the longest serving 20th Century British Prime Minister?

98. At whose court did the famous Persian poet Amir Khusro live?

99. Who was the President of India when Prime Minister Indira Gandhi declared a state of emergency in 1975?

100. Who is known as 'The Father of American Constitution'?

DID YOU KNOW?

- John F. Kennedy, at the age of 43, was the youngest US President.
- Margaret Thatcher was the longest serving British Prime Minister of the 20th Century. She was in office for 11 years and 208 days.

LANGUAGE & LITERATURE

1. Which is the longest epic in the world literature?
2. Who wrote 'The Jungle Book'?
3. Which is the most widely spoken language in the world?
4. What is the principal language of Kerala?
5. In which language are the most newspapers published in India?
6. Which is the oldest surviving language in the world?
7. Who is the author of 'Godan'?
8. Who wrote 'The Arabian Nights'?
9. From which language does the word 'ketchup' come?
10. Which is the most used word in the English language?
11. Which book has been printed in the maximum number of languages?
12. In which language was our national anthem, *Jana-gana-mana*, originally composed?
13. In which language was our national song, *Vande Mataram*, originally composed?
14. What was the pen-name of Charles Lutwidge Dodgson?
15. Who wrote 'The Animal Farm'?
16. Who is the author of 'Gitanjali'?
17. What was the pen-name of Dhanpat Rai?
18. Which book of Salman Rushdie was banned by all Muslim countries including India?

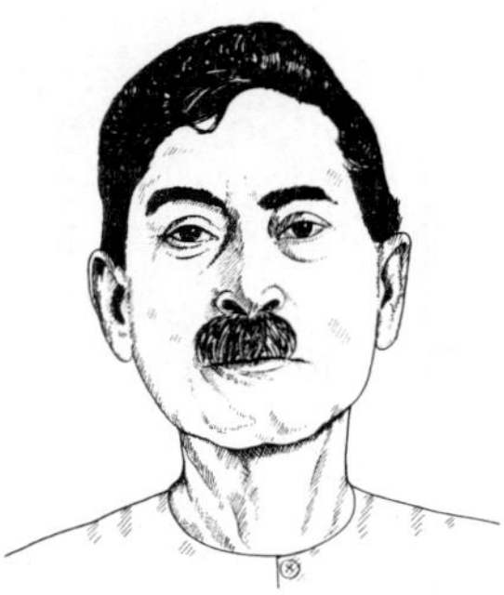

19. For which novel did Arundhati Roy win the Booker Prize in 1997?
20. In which country are more languages spoken than in any other country?

DID YOU KNOW?

- Of the 7,000 languages and dialects spoken in the world, 845 are Indian.
- The world's best-selling fiction writer is the late Agatha Christie (UK). She wrote 78 crime novels and sold about 2 billion copies worldwide in 44 languages.

21. Which author's collection of short stories is titled 'Mansarover'?

22. What is a person who writes and edits dictionaries called?
23. What is a person who loves and collects books called?
24. What was the real name of Valmiki, the author of *Ramayana*?
25. Who wrote 'A Suitable Boy'?
26. Who is the author of 'Anand Math'?
27. In which language are the Buddhist sacred scriptures written?
28. Who is known as 'The Grand Old Man of Indian English Fiction'?
29. In which book our national song, *Vande Mataram*, was first published?
30. Who wrote 'India Divided'?
31. Which two capitals feature in Dickens' 'A Tale of Two Cities'?
32. Which Hindi writer was known as 'Upanyas Samrat'?

33. Who authored the famous Punjabi novel 'Pinjar'?
34. In which languages did the poet Mirza Ghalib write?
35. Which is the longest English novel in India?
36. How many languages are listed as the official languages in the Constitution of India?
37. Which one of Salman Rushdie's novels won 'The Booker of Bookers' award in 1993 (i.e. the best novel of the last 25 years)?
38. Which famous English poet wrote his best works after he became blind?
39. Who is known as 'The Father of English Poetry'?
40. Who is the author of the famous novel 'Dr. Zhivago'?

DID YOU KNOW?

- The term philosophy comes from the Greek 'philosophia', which means 'love of wisdom'.
- The late Osho Rajneesh is considered the most prolific non-fiction writer. He has credited with over 650 books translated into 32 languages.

ART & CULTURE

1. Who painted the famous painting *Mona Lisa*?

2. Name the folk-dance of Assam.
3. Which musical instrument does Hari Prasad Chaurasia play?
4. In which country did the violin originate?
5. Which Indian state do you associate with *Garba*?
6. What is a lady ballet dancer called?
7. In which Indian state is the 'Surajkund Mela' annually held?
8. Name the festival of Kerala during which boat races are held.

9. Which is the most ancient musical instrument of India?
10. What is the traditional costume of Japan called?
11. Which is the famous classical dance form of Kerala?
12. Which musical instrument is played by the leader of an orchestra?
13. Which musical instrument does Ustaad Amjad Ali Khan play?
14. Which Indian state do you associate with *Lavni*?
15. Which Indian classical instrument normally has one hundred strings?
16. Which classical dance of India is named after a village in Andhra Pradesh?
17. Which dance form is Birju Maharaj renowned for?

18. Which country do you associate with *Samba* dance?
19. Which museum will you have to visit to see Leonardo da Vinci's *Mona Lisa*?
20. What is the short stick that a music conductor carries called?

DID YOU KNOW?

- While performing Kuchipudi, the dancers themselves used to sing.
- Gwalior in Madhya Pradesh, was so advanced in music during the Mughal period that out of 36 musicians at Akbar's court, as many as 15 came from Gwalior.

Religion & Mythology

1. Who was the founder of Sikhism?
2. Where was the Lord Buddha born?
3. Where was the Prophet Muhammad born?
4. Which is the oldest Hindu epic?
5. Where is the Sun Temple in India?
6. Which is the most sacred book of Islam?
7. Which is the largest religion in the world?
8. Which is the fastest growing religion in the world?

9. Who founded the city of Amritsar?
10. Who was crucified when he was just 33?
11. Which Hindu god has a *vahan* named Nandi?
12. Where was the Guru Nanak born?
13. What is the name most frequently adopted by the popes?
14. Which Indian fair is celebrated once in every twelve years?
15. What is the holy journey to Mecca made by the Muslims called?

16. What is a Tibetan monk usually known as?
17. Which Hindu god has the head of an elephant?
18. Which goddess is worshipped on the Diwali festival?
19. For how many days was the Battle of Kurukshetra fought?
20. Who is credited to have shown the way for the river Ganga from heaven to the earth?

DID YOU KNOW?

- Christianity is the world's largest religion followed by about 33% of the world's population.
- Islam is the fastest growing religion in the world. Approximately 20% of the world's population follows Islam.

RELIGION & MYTHOLOGY

21. In which country is the religion *Shintoism* followed?
22. What is the name of the month during which Muslims fast?
23. Where was the Jesus Christ born?
24. What is the meaning of *Bhagavadgita*?
25. Who built the Golden Temple in Amritsar?
26. Where did the Lord Buddha attain enlightenment?
27. Which is the largest temple in India?
28. Which is the largest church in India?
29. Which is the largest church in the world?
30. Which is the largest mosque in the world?
31. Where is the Amarnath Cave?
32. Which is the richest temple in India?
33. Who among the Pandavas killed Duryodhana?
34. Who was the founder of a new religion *Din-e-Elahi*?
35. What is the meaning of *Din-e-Elahi*?
36. According to the Hindu mythology, who is the father of Lord Ganesha?
37. Where is the Wailing Wall situated?
38. Which brother of Ravana joined Rama against his own brother?
39. Which saint is regarded as the first Christian Missionary to come to India?
40. On which day of the week, do Muslims go to the mosque to offer special prayer?

DID YOU KNOW?

- Hajj, the annual pilgrimage to Mecca, Saudi Arabia, attracts an average of 2 million Muslims a year.
- Hair, offered by devotees at the Tirupati Temple in Andhra Pradesh, are sold in auction, earning over Rs. 4 crores annually for the temple.

RELIGION & MYTHOLOGY

41. Which is the most sacred pilgrim-centre of Muslims?

42. Where is the Jagannath Temple in India?
43. Who worship in a Fire Temple?
44. Which Hindu god has a rat as his *vahan*?
45. What does the word *Sikh* mean?
46. What is the meaning of *Islam*?
47. To which religion does the *Digambara* sect belong?
48. To which religion do the sects *Sunnis* and *Shias* belong?
49. Which religious faith is associated with the Lotus Temple in New Delhi?
50. In *Mahabharata*, who is the only daughter of Dhritarashtra?
51. Which Sikh Guru compiled the *Guru Granth Sahib*?

52. Which Sikh Guru complied the *Adi Granth*?
53. Which is the oldest of four *Vedas*?
54. Who is the protector and preserver of the world according to the Hindu mythology?
55. In which country are the ruins of the largest Hindu temple complex, the Angkor Vat, found?
56. Which monkey king helped Rama to fight Ravana?
57. How are Zoroastrians more popularly known?
58. At which muni's Ashram were Lava-Kusha, the twin sons of Rama and Sita, born?
59. Name the saint in whose honour the *Urs* fair is held in Ajmer every year.
60. The *Rath Yatra* at Puri is celebrated in the honour of which Hindu deity?

DID YOU KNOW?

- The 'badi-deg' (big vessel), presented by Mughal Emperor Akbar to the tomb of Khwaja Muin-ud-din Chishti at Ajmer, is the largest cooking vessel in the world. It could cook 4,000 kg of food at a time, enough to serve 12,000 people.

MONUMENTS & OTHER STRUCTURES

1. Which is the tallest statue in the world?
2. Where is the Eiffel Tower?
3. Which is the highest gateway in India?
4. Which is the tallest minaret in the world?
5. Where is the rock garden in India?
6. Who designed the Taj Mahal?
7. Which is the largest residential house in India?
8. Which gate in Delhi is called 'Khooni Darwaza'?
9. Which is the longest railway platform in the world?
10. Which is the tallest building in the world?
11. Which is the tallest building in India?
12. Who designed the Parliament House of India?
13. Which place is the official residence of the British royal family?
14. Where is the Dolls Museum in India?
15. How many triangular sides does a pyramid have?
16. Which Indian city has the most monuments?
17. Which is the tallest statue in India?
18. Which is the highest dam in India?
19. Name the building which houses the US Defence Ministry in Washington, DC.
20. Which Indian monument is famous for depicting the history of the British rule in India?

DID YOU KNOW?

- The 32 m high statue of Lord Hanumana in Nandura, Maharashtra, is the tallest statue in India.
- The DLF City, a residential and business complex spread over 2,800 acres at New Gurgaon in Haryana, is Asia's largest private township.

MONUMENTS & OTHER STRUCTURES

21. Which is the tallest tower in the world?
22. Which is the world's largest office building?
23. Which is the largest prison in India?
24. Who designed the Eiffel Tower?
25. Where do you find the ruins of Colosseum?
26. Which country gifted the Statue of Liberty to the United States?
27. What is the height of Qutub Minar?
28. Who was the creator of the famous Rock Garden in Chandigarh?
29. On which monument do you find the *Amar Jawan Jyoti* always burning?
30. Where is the Salar Jung Museum in India?
31. Where are the Petronas Twin Towers situated?
32. Where is the Tower of Victory in India?
33. Which is the largest cantilever bridge in India?
34. Which is the longest bridge in the world?
35. Where do you find the Humayun's Tomb?
36. Which four American Presidents are sculptured on Mount Rushmore in South Dakota, USA?

37. Which is the largest airport in the world?
38. Where is the Indian museum, the oldest museum in India, situated?
39. Which famous war memorial was designed by Sir Edwin Lutyens?
40. Who completed the Qutub Minar after the death of Qutub-ud-din Aibak?

DID YOU KNOW?

- ❖ The Eiffel Tower of Paris, built in 1889, used over 7,000 tonnes of iron.
- ❖ The Pentagon, which houses the US Defence Department's offices in Virginia, USA, is the largest office building in the world. Its five storeys enclose a floor area of 6,04,000 sq. m and have 7,754 windows.

MISCELLANEOUS

1. Which country has the world's largest army?
2. What is the symbol of Air India?
3. What does the *Chakra* in our national flag signify?
4. Which is the largest democratic country in the world?
5. Which is the largest permanent exhibition ground in Asia?
6. What is our national song?
7. Who is considered to be the first citizen of India?
8. Which is the fastest train in India?
9. When is the Teachers' Day celebrated?
10. What is capital punishment?
11. Which country's flag has 50 stars?
12. Which is the largest library in India?
13. Which is the largest library in the world?
14. How many sheets are there in a ream of paper?
15. What is the stamp collecting hobby called?
16. What is a place where money is manufactured called?
17. What is the name of the first supercomputer made in India?
18. What is the name of the garden situated in the premises of the Rashtrapati Bhavan?
19. In how much time should our national anthem be sung and completed?
20. Which Indian bank has the largest number of branches?

DID YOU KNOW?

- The State Bank of India holds the world record of most branches—over 9,000 in India and abroad.
- The most common method of execution in the world is by firing squad, practiced in 73 countries worldwide, followed by hanging, which is practiced in 58 countries.

MISCELLANEOUS

21. Which country was the first to issue the postage stamp?
22. Which is the longest road in India?
23. Which city in India has the largest number of motor vehicles?
24. Who is the supreme commander of the Indian armed forces?
25. What does the letter 'H' stand for on a pencil?
26. How many spokes are there in the *Chakra* of our national flag?
27. What is the full form of VPP?
28. Which two rivers have been named in our national anthem?
29. Which is India's principal bank?
30. What is the national emblem of Pakistan?
31. Which is the most common surname in the world?
32. How many days does February have in a leap year?
33. What is meant by flag at half-mast?
34. What is Ferozabad famous for?
35. Where did India conduct its first underground nuclear test?
36. Which device connects a computer to a telephone line?
37. What term is commonly used for a photocopying machine?
38. What is the minimum age prescribed for a candidate to be elected to the office of the President of India?
39. Name the clock situated on the tower of the British Parliament in London.
40. What mathematical notation did India give to the world?

DID YOU KNOW?

- Around 5,000 daily newspapers are published in India in about 100 languages and dialects.
- The American Philatelic Society, founded in 1886, is the largest non-profit society in the world for stamp collectors and postal historians. It has over 55,000 members in more than 110 countries.

MISCELLANEOUS

41. Which was India's first newspaper?

42. Which is the largest slum in India?
43. Which is the world's fastest train?
44. What is Geneva famous for?
45. What is the full form of ISBN?
46. Which city is called the Financial Capital of India?
47. Which country is considered the birthplace of *Pizza*?
48. What does the saffron colour in our national flag signify?
49. What does the white colour in our national flag signify?
50. What does the green colour in our national flag signify?
51. Which is the world's most polluted major city?
52. What is a sweet dish eaten at the end of a meal called?
53. What was the first animal to go into the space?
54. Which is the senior-most regiment in the Indian Army?
55. What is a cashier who pays out money in a bank called?
56. In which year did the Microsoft Company introduce the first Windows-based operating system?
57. Where do you find the Brindavan Gardens in India?
58. Which is the highest civilian award in India?
59. Which is the highest gallantry award in India?
60. Which Asian country has the largest railway network?

DID YOU KNOW?

- Indian Railways with over 15.75 lakh employees, is the largest employer in the world.
- Balamurli Ambati of India, the world's youngest doctor, got his degree from Mount Sinai School of Medicine, New York in 1995 at the age of 17.

MISCELLANEOUS

61. Which country has the largest postal network in the world?
62. Which is the oldest university in Britain?
63. Which city in India is famous for its snake park?
64. Which is the most prestigious award in the world?
65. Which company is the world's largest computer manufacturer?
66. Who assassinated Mahatma Gandhi?
67. What is a shed/building in which aircraft are kept called?
68. Which is the oldest existing English daily in India?
69. Who built the Grand Trunk Road?
70. Which country won/shared the most number of Nobel Prizes?
71. ISI is an intelligence agency of which country?
72. What is the full form of ISI?
73. Where are the headquarters of the Red Cross?
74. What is a person who cuts and sells meat called?
75. What are the three words inscribed on the national emblem of India?
76. Which country has the world's largest fishing industry?
77. To which country does the Republican Party belong?
78. Which state is the largest producer of sugar in India?
79. What is the other name for International Bank for Reconstruction and Development (IBRD)?
80. Where is the world's highest battleground in the world?

DID YOU KNOW?

- The Silicon Valley near San Francisco, USA, has the world's greatest concentration of electronics firms.
- Tathagat Avatar Tulsi, born on Sept. 9, 1987 in Bihar, is the youngest post-graduate in India. He passed his M.Sc. in 1999 at 12 years and 2 months only.

MISCELLANEOUS

81. Which country awards the Nobel Prizes?
82. How many Indians have received the Nobel Prizes so far?
83. Which is the oldest surviving airline in the world?
84. Which country's Constitution is the longest in the world?
85. In which country is Encyclopedia Britannica published?
86. Where are the headquarters of the UNO?
87. Which material is generally used for making our national flag?
88. Into how many zones is the Indian railway divided?
89. Which Indian city is famous for the brassware industry?
90. What is the full form of AIIMS?
91. If John Bull represents England, who represents the USA?
92. Which country leads the world in the production of coffee?
93. What is the tax imposed on import or export of goods called?
94. How many lions are there in our national emblem?
95. When were the Twin Towers of World Trade Centre (New York) destroyed?
96. What is the minimum age for becoming a member of the Lok Sabha?
97. What is the Parliament of Japan called?
98. Which state is the largest producer of rice in India?
99. In which field is the Bhatnagar Award given in India?
100. Which award in mathematics is considered to be the equivalent of the Nobel Prize?

DID YOU KNOW?

- Dr. P. Venugopal performed the first successful human heart transplant at AIIMS, New Delhi in 1994.
- 2,823 people were killed as a result of the terrorist attack on the World Trade Centre, New York, USA, on September 11, 2001.

MISCELLANEOUS

101. What kind of leaf is there on the Canadian flag?

102. What is the official language of Iran?
103. Which company is the largest manufacturer of bicycles in the world?
104. To which country does the Nazi Party belong?
105. What is the study of human population known as?
106. On which date are the Nobel Prizes awarded each year?
107. Which country is the largest producer of wheat in the world?
108. What is the full form of IGNOU?
109. Which forest is associated with Robin Hood?
110. Which was the first country in the world to give women the right to vote?
111. Which country has the most number of neighbours touching its border?
112. Which country operates the Lufthansa Airlines?
113. What is the ratio of width of our national flag to its length?
114. What is an order to a person to appear in a lawcourt called?
115. Is the President of India eligible for re-election?
116. Which country's flag has been given the name 'The Stars and the Strips'?
117. What is the first hour of every sitting of the Lok Sabha called?
118. What is a place where weapons and explosives are made or stored called?
119. What was the name of the first electric train of India?
120. Which is the longest passenger route on the Indian Railways?

DID YOU KNOW?

- New Zealand was the first country to allow women to vote.
- Hotmail was the first free e-mail service, conceived and launched by Sabeer Bhatia in 1996. Hotmail is now the property of Microsoft Inc. with over 110 million subscribers from almost all countries of the world.

MISCELLANEOUS

121. Which street is famous for the Mumbai Stock Exchange?
122. When is the World's AIDS Day celebrated?
123. What is the full form of LTTE?
124. Which is the longest train in India?
125. In which discipline was the last Nobel Prize introduced in 1968?
126. What is the official language of Brazil?
127. How many centimetres are there in one inch?
128. How many kilometres are equal to one mile?
129. How many grams are there in one pound?
130. How many litres are there in one gallon?
131. Who maintains the land-records of a village?
132. Which country operates the QANTAS Airlines?
133. Which country has the zero birth rate?
134. Which Indian city is associated with the aircraft industry?
135. Where is the Indian Military Academy?
136. Where is the National Defence Academy?
137. Which company was involved in the Bhopal Gas Tragedy?
138. To whom the President of India addresses his hand-written resignation when he resigns from the office?
139. In which field is the Feroz Gandhi Award given?
140. Where are the headquarters of the International Court of Justice?

DID YOU KNOW?

- The greatest amount paid by a single cheque in the history of banking was £ 2,47,46,55,000.
- On December 3, 1984, the leakage of methyl isocyanate, a poisonous gas, from the Union Carbide pesticide plant near Bhopal, killed more than 6,300 people.

MISCELLANEOUS

141. What is the name of the plane that the President of USA uses officially?
142. Which country gives the Magsaysay Awards?
143. Where are the headquarters of the Interpol?
144. Name the street which is the site of official residence of the British Prime Minister.
145. When is the UN Day celebrated each year?
146. What is the full form of SAARC?
147. What is the full form of CTBT?
148. In which field is the Borlaug Award given?
149. Which country's Parliament is called *Dumas*?
150. Which international organization has received three Nobel Peace Prizes?
151. Who appoints the Governor of each state of India?
152. In which year was the term World Wide Web introduced?
153. What does the term 'fourth estate' refer to?
154. Which company introduced the world's first microprocessor?
155. When do we celebrate the World Environment Day?
156. Which street is famous for the Stock Exchange Market in New York?
157. Name the only US President who has elected to four terms.
158. Which gas was responsible for the Bhopal gas tragedy?
159. In which year did India conduct its first underground test at Pokhran, Rajasthan?
160. Under which article of the Indian Constitution, the President of India can declare emergency in any state of India?

DID YOU KNOW?

- Google, with over 3 billion web pages, is the largest internet search engine in the world.
- Dr. M.C. Modi of India has performed the most eye operations in the world—a total of 6,10,564 between 1943 and 1993.

Picture Quiz

Identify the following famous personalities:

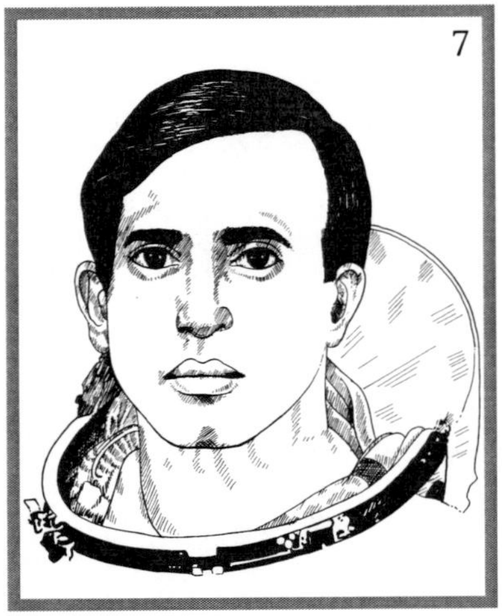

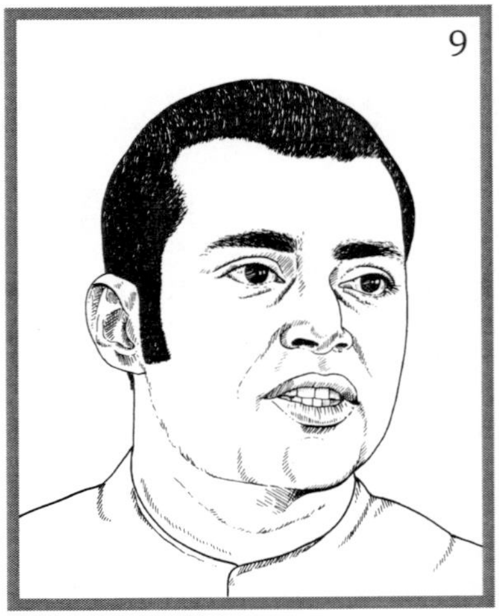

ANSWERS

ANIMALS

1. Cheetah (110 km/h)
2. Elephant (6,500 kg)
3. Blue whale (1,35,000 kg)
4. Giraffe (5.5 m)
5. Ostrich (150 kg)
6. Bee hummingbird (3 g)
7. Bat
8. Kiwi
9. Giant panda
10. Anaconda (250 kg)
11. Reticulated python (10 m)
12. Siberian tiger
13. Ivory
14. Joey
15. Pearls
16. Dove
17. Taipan
18. Antarctica
19. Ostrich (70 km/h)
20. Gir National Park (Gujarat)
21. Whale shark
22. A tail
23. Hibernation
24. Elephant
25. Komodo dragon
26. Ostrich, Penguin, Kiwi, Emu, Rhea, etc.
27. Eight
28. Paragnas (West Bengal)
29. Kaziranga National Park (Assam)
30. Ghana Bird Sanctuary (Rajasthan)
31. Gills
32. Blue
33. Octopus
34. Hummingbird
35. Nectar
36. Only one
37. Horse
38. Saltwater crocodile
39. Bison
40. Lizard
41. King cobra
42. Platypus
43. China
44. Sailfish (110 km/h)
45. Ostrich
46. Ornithology
47. Spoonbill
48. Junagarh (Gujarat)
49. Keratin
50. Swift (200 km/h)
51. Cheetahs
52. Hexagonal
53. Bald eagle
54. Hippopotamus
55. Bamboo leaves
56. Drones
57. Stallion
58. Pelican
59. In a tunnel in riverbank
60. Wild ass
61. Arctic tern
62. Polar bear
63. Beaver
64. Dragonfly (75 km/h)
65. Rattlesnake
66. Stag
67. Harpy eagle
68. On its feet
69. Australia
70. Giant anteater (60 cm long)
71. Wandering albatross (wingspan 3.3 m)
72. Whale shark
73. Crane
74. They just glide
75. A species of bat
76. Jorhat (Assam)
77. South America
78. Orang-utan
79. Australia
80. Kakapo (found in New Zealand)
81. Shark
82. Sloth
83. Koala
84. Gila monster
85. Milking
86. Feathers
87. Thread snake (10 cm only)
88. Moose (also known as Elk)
89. About 3 g only
90. Mandla (Madhya Pradesh)
91. Kiwi
92. Cormorant
93. Andean condor
94. Mute swan (18 kg)
95. Australia
96. Spiders
97. Capybara
98. Tyrannosaurus rex
99. Entomology
100. Ethology

PLANTS & TREES

1. Rafflesia
2. China
3. Chlorophyll
4. Rice
5. Grapes
6. Olive
7. Mango
8. Apple
9. Mushroom
10. Seeds
11. Brinjal
12. Bamboo
13. Corpse flower
14. China rose
15. Sunderbans
16. Redwood (over 100 m high and 8 m thick)
17. Citrus fruits (oranges, lemons, etc.)
18. The Amazon rainforest
19. Death cap
20. Quinine

THE HUMAN BODY

1. Liver (1.6 kg)
2. 206
3. 72
4. Vitamin A
5. 37°C
6. Skin
7. Common cold
8. O, A, B, AB
9. Haemoglobin
10. 20
11. 450 ml
12. Marrow
13. Goitre
14. Ribs
15. Rabies (also known as Hydrophobia)
16. 6/6 (metres)
17. Leprosy
18. WBC
19. Vitamin C
20. About 5.5 litres
21. Vitamin K
22. Stirrup (found in the ear)
23. Femur (found in the thigh)
24. Group O
25. Group AB
26. Spinal cord
27. Dermatologist
28. Brain
29. Rickets
30. Cholesterol
31. AIDS
32. Psychiatrist
33. Diabetes
34. Tuberculosis
35. Liver
36. Recipe (meaning take)
37. Muscles
38. 1.5 kg
39. 30
40. Bone marrow
41. Amnesia
42. Iris
43. Acupuncture
44. Lungs
45. Melanin
46. Cerebrum
47. Pancreas
48. Liver
49. Cardiologist
50. Thyroid gland
51. Intestines
52. Within the ear
53. Eyes
54. To maintain sugar level in the body
55. Kidney failure

GENERAL SCIENCE

1. Milky Way
2. Saturn
3. Crater
4. Seven
5. Sun
6. Compressed Natural Gas
7. 8 minutes
8. Thomas Alva Edison
9. Diamond
10. Blue
11. Expands
12. Jupiter
13. Yuri Gagarin
14. Stethoscope
15. Sputnik 1
16. Phosphorus
17. Mercury
18. Neil Armstrong
19. Steam
20. Teflon
21. Hydrogen
22. Light

ANSWERS

23. Arachnophobia (Phobia of spiders)
24. HIV
25. Filament
26. Carbon dioxide
27. Ozone
28. E.G. Otis
29. Radar
30. Sodium chloride
31. Blood cancer
32. 0°C
33. 100°C
34. Acquired Immune Deficiency Syndrome
35. Orbit
36. Charles Darwin
37. Methane
38. Carbon monoxide
39. Distance in space
40. Odometer
41. Kalpana Chawla
42. 24 Carats
43. Alfred Bernhard Nobel
44. Calcium carbonate
45. Charles Darwin
46. Carbon dioxide
47. Nothing can travel faster than light.
48. Black
49. Germany
50. Nicolaus Copernicus
51. Knot
52. Johannes Gutenberg
53. Edwin Aldrin
54. Atom bomb
55. Brahmagupta
56. Hydrogen
57. Copper
58. White surface
59. Transformer
60. Periscope
61. Silicon
62. Benjamin Franklin
63. Michael Faraday
64. Sulphuric acid
65. To escape from the Radar
66. Neon
67. ECG (Electrocardiograph)
68. 1969
69. Watt
70. Jagdish Chandra Bose
71. Thumba (Kerala)
72. Thomas Alva Edison
73. Earth
74. J.B. Dunlop
75. Indian Space Research Organization
76. National Aeronautics and Space Administration (USA)
77. Carburetor
78. Diopter
79. Hubble
80. Black box
81. Cosmonaut
82. Eye
83. Mars
84. Nitrogen
85. 1.5 volts
86. Mercury
87. Seismograph
88. Neil Armstrong
89. Global Positioning System
90. Elliptical
91. Galileo Galilei
92. Wood
93. Yeast
94. Medicine
95. Optics
96. Kite
97. Anemometer
98. Apollo 11
99. Radium and Polonium
100. Aryabhatta
101. Mercury and Venus
102. Tungsten
103. Edward Jenner
104. Alexander Fleming
105. Albert Einstein
106. A meteor
107. Decibel
108. Sikorsky
109. C. Cokerell
110. 1961
111. Homi Jahangir Bhabha
112. Transponder
113. Sirius
114. Aryabhatta
115. Epidemic
116. Lactic acid
117. Proxima Centauri
118. Michael Faraday
119. Echo
120. Ecology
121. Mercury
122. On the moon
123. William Harvey
124. Veterinarian
125. 332 km/s
126. 3,00,000 km/s
127. Water
128. Brass
129. Nitrous oxide
130. Sulphuric and Nitric acids
131. Meteorology
132. Helium and Hydrogen
133. Blood pressure
134. Aluminium
135. Aspirin
136. Cosmic Year
137. Dr. Har Gobind Khorana
138. Max Planck
139. Storm
140. Cape Kennedy, Florida

SPORTS

1. Five
2. Football
3. Olympics
4. 64
5. Five
6. 1983
7. Zero score
8. Baseball
9. India
10. Black
11. 22 yards (66 feet)
12. 24 feet
13. 10 feet
14. Mumbai
15. Empty hand
16. Arena
17. Pele
18. 19
19. Indira Gandhi Indoor Stadium
20. Brazil (Five)
21. Greece
22. Polo
23. Chess
24. Boxing
25. Table tennis
26. Kapil Dev
27. Arjun Award
28. Australia (Three)
29. Sumo
30. Dhyan Chand
31. Yellow
32. Polo
33. Martina Navratilova
34. Swimming
35. Football
36. Greece
37. Vishwanathan Anand
38. Mansur Ali Khan Pataudi
39. Dronacharya Award
40. Willow
41. Durand Cup
42. 70 minutes
43. P.T. Usha
44. Tennis
45. Iran
46. Deep Blue
47. Eden Gardens (Kolkata)
48. Weightlifting
49. Uruguay
50. Puck
51. Ice-hockey
52. 1896
53. Sachin Tendulkar
54. Football
55. Federation International de Football Association
56. Snooker
57. Brian Lara (400)
58. Brazil
59. Mike Tyson
60. Athens (Greece)
61. Bull fighting
62. World Cup Soccer
63. Tennis
64. Sir Don Bradman
65. Cassius Clay
66. Lucknow
67. Mahesh Bhupati
68. Carl Lewis (1984 & 1988)
69. None
70. Prakash Padukone
71. 16 days
72. Karnam Malleswari
73. Major Rajyavardhan Singh Rathore
74. 101
75. Strahov Stadium (Prague)
76. Cricket
77. Mansur Ali Khan Pataudi
78. Allahabad (UP)
79. Vijayalakshmi Subbraman
80. Javed Miandad
81. Germany
82. Basketball
83. Baron Pierre de Coubertine
84. Badminton
85. Muhammad Ali
86. Chetan Sharma

ANSWERS

87. 42 km 195 m
88. England
89. Mohd. Azharuddin
90. Carl Lewis
91. 1928
92. Fibre glass
93. 1904
94. Cassius Clay (Muhammad Ali)
95. Lausanne (Switzerland)

HISTORY

1. Babar
2. Adolf Hitler
3. Portuguese
4. Meerut (UP)
5. Nadir Shah
6. Jodha Bai
7. 1950
8. Guru Arjun Dev
9. Bahadur Shah Zafar
10. Jahangir
11. Iltutmish
12. 1952
13. Mumbai
14. Vladimir Lenin
15. Alexander the Great
16. Greek
17. General Dyer
18. Surat (Gujarat)
19. India and Pakistan
20. Agra
21. Humayun
22. Maurya Empire
23. Amritsar (Punjab)
24. 1945
25. St. Helena
26. Sambhaji
27. Shah Jahan
28. Salim
29. Bahadur Shah Zafar
30. Sabarmati Ashram
31. Sepoy Mutiny
32. Sukhdev and Rajguru
33. Siraj-ud-Daulah
34. Humayun
35. Queen Victoria
36. Chandragupta Maurya
37. Bindusara
38. 1905
39. Attack on Pearl Harbour by Japan
40. Panipat (Haryana)
41. The Liberal Party
42. Lord Curzon
43. Duke of Wellington
44. The First Battle of Panipat
45. Pharaohs
46. England and France
47. Porus
48. Khwaja Salim Chishti
49. 1885
50. Sardar Vallabhbhai Patel
51. Harry Truman
52. Nadir Shah
53. Bahadur Shah Zafar
54. America and Great Britain
55. The League of Nations (1920)

GEOGRAPHY

1. Ganga
2. Nile
3. Amazon
4. Yangtze River (China)
5. Thar
6. Gobi (Mongolia–China)
7. Sahara
8. Jog Falls
9. Angel Falls
10. Sunderbans
11. Mount Everest
12. Nanga Parbat
13. Pacific
14. Lake Superior
15. Caspian Sea
16. About 70%
17. Europe
18. Mawsynram (Meghalaya)
19. Dead Sea
20. Coral Sea
21. Goa
22. Rajasthan
23. Mumbai
24. Kolkata
25. Chandigarh
26. Jammu & Kashmir
27. Dehradun
28. 10 years
29. 28 States & 7 Union Territories
30. Tatanagar
31. Chennai
32. Varanasi
33. Uttar Pradesh
34. Sikkim
35. New Delhi
36. China
37. Akbar
38. The Abode of Snow
39. Kanpur
40. Chilka Lake (Orissa)
41. Russia
42. Vatican City (Rome)
43. Nippon
44. 8,850 m
45. Africa
46. China
47. Dead Sea
48. Canberra
49. Christopher Columbus
50. Egypt
51. Holland
52. Red Indians
53. Bhutan
54. Eater of raw meat
55. London
56. Japan
57. Mawsynram (Meghalaya)
58. Atacama Desert
59. New York
60. Ferdinand Magellan
61. Gujarat (1,600 km)
62. Marianas Trench
63. Cartographer
64. Switzerland
65. West Bengal
66. Great Britain
67. Hooghly
68. Jerusalem
69. Ladakh
70. Uttar Pradesh (7)
71. Mozambique
72. Marina Beach
73. Africa
74. From the North
75. Amazon
76. Iran
77. Assam, Arunachal Pradesh, Meghalaya, Manipur, Mizoram, Nagaland and Tripura
78. Australia
79. Allahabad
80. Patna
81. Tokyo
82. Pamirs (Tibet)
83. Iceberg
84. Beijing
85. California
86. Jhelum
87. Greenland
88. Madhya Pradesh
89. South America
90. Jaipur
91. Dutch
92. Haryana
93. Jammu & Kashmir
94. Tundra
95. Athens
96. South Africa
97. England, Scotland, Northern Ireland and Wales
98. Venezuela
99. Vasco da Gama
100. Indira Gandhi Nahar
101. Canada
102. Lake Baikal (Russia)
103. Gold mines
104. Damodar River
105. Shanghai
106. Canada and USA
107. Paris
108. Tripura
109. Grand Canal (China)
110. McMohan Line
111. Egypt
112. San Francisco (California)
113. K2 (Godwin–Austen)
114. 50
115. Canada
116. Siachen Glacier
117. Oxbow
118. Sutlej
119. Cochin
120. Suez Canal
121. Alaska
122. Nile
123. Mansarovar
124. Australia
125. Grand Canyon
126. Calicut (now Kozhikode)
127. Zambezi River
128. Palestine
129. Tiber
130. Suez Canal
131. River Huang He
132. Darjeeling
133. Allahabad
134. Peru
135. Ghana
136. Goa
137. Amazon
138. Jog Falls
139. India and Sri Lanka

ANSWERS

140. Himalayas
141. Arunachal Pradesh
142. Roald Amundsen
143. Arizona (USA)
144. Colorado
145. California (USA)
146. Andes (South America)
147. Alps
148. Urals
149. USA–Canada border
150. Hong Kong
151. Uttar Pradesh
152. 5,600 km
153. Sharavati
154. Indus
155. Madagascar
156. Andaman and Nicobar Islands
157. Dehradun
158. Nilgiri Hills
159. Alaska
160. Igneous

CINEMA

1. Satyajit Ray
2. Bhanu Athaiya
3. Ramesh Sippi
4. Alam Ara
5. The Jazz Singer
6. Jurassic Park
7. James Cameron
8. India
9. Dilip Kumar
10. Amitabh Bachchan
11. Sir Ben Kingsley
12. Oscar Awards
13. Coolie
14. Steven Spielberg
15. Walt Disney (26 Oscars)
16. Mehboob Khan
17. Dada Saheb Phalke
18. Lata Mangeshkar
19. Gandhi (over 3,00,000 extras in the funeral process)
20. Naya Din Nai Raat

FAMOUS PERSONALITIES

1. Rabindranath Tagore
2. Dr. Rajendra Prasad
3. Walt Disney
4. Dr. B.R. Ambedkar
5. Rabindranath Tagore
6. Bankim Chandra Chatterji
7. Mother Teresa
8. Dr. S. Radhakrishnan's
9. Thomas Alva Edison
10. Rajiv Gandhi
11. Pran
12. Bachendri Pal
13. London
14. Bhagat Singh
15. Christiaan Barnard
16. Junko Tabei
17. Reita Faria (1966)
18. George Washington
19. Sir Edwin Lutyens
20. Mahatma Gandhi
21. Santosh Yadav
22. Abraham Lincoln
23. Dr. Iqbal
24. Kiran Bedi
25. New Zealand
26. Dr. A.P.J. Abdul Kalam
27. Lal Bahadur Shastri
28. Madan Mohan Malviya
29. Rabindranath Tagore
30. Gulzari Lal Nanda
31. Rabindranath Tagore
32. Mahatma Gandhi
33. Sirimavo Bandaranaike
34. Sarojini Naidu
35. Tansen
36. Sir Winston Churchill
37. Rajiv Gandhi
38. Chanakya
39. Rajiv Gandhi
40. Salim Ali
41. Florence Nightingale
42. Salim Ali
43. Jean Henri Dunant
44. Sher Shah Suri
45. Benazir Bhutto
46. A.O. Hume
47. Porbandar (Gujarat)
48. Marie Curie
49. Dr. Zakir Husain (about 2 years)
50. M. Fatima Beevi
51. W.C. Bonerjee
52. Florence Nightingale
53. Lal Bahadur Shastri
54. Louise Braille
55. Jyoti Basu
56. R.K. Laxman
57. James Augustus Hickey
58. Gwalior (MP)
59. Lala Lajpat Rai
60. Tipu Sultan
61. Margaret Thatcher
62. Le Corbusier
63. Neelam Sanjiva Reddy
64. Sir Syed Ahmad Khan
65. Abdul Ghaffar Khan
66. Varanasi (UP)
67. Raja Ram Mohan Rai
68. Mother Teresa
69. Abdul Ghaffar Khan
70. Dr. P. Venugopal
71. Sir George Everest
72. King Solomon
73. Annie Besant
74. Lord Irwin
75. Austria
76. Dr. Amartya Sen
77. Udham Singh
78. Mahatma Gandhi
79. Kalpana Chawla
80. Rabindranath Tagore
81. Arati Shah
82. Martin Luther King
83. Germany
84. Charan Singh
85. Mother Teresa
86. John Adams
87. Rudyard Kipling
88. Lord William Bentinck
89. Swami Dayanand Saraswati
90. Aristotle
91. 1564
92. Adolf Hitler
93. Sir Isaac Pitman
94. Dr. Nagendra Prasad
95. Rabindranath Tagore
96. Dadabhai Naoroji
97. Margaret Thatcher
98. Ala-ud-din Khilji
99. Fakhruddin Ali Ahmad
100. James Madison

LANGUAGE & LITERATURE

1. Mahabharata
2. Rudyard Kipling
3. Mandarin Chinese (Standard Chinese)
4. Malayalam
5. Hindi
6. Tamil
7. Premchand
8. Sir Richard Burton
9. Chinese
10. The Bible
11. Bible
12. Bengali
13. Sanskrit
14. Lewis Carroll
15. George Orwell
16. Rabindranath Tagore
17. Premchand
18. The Satanic Verses
19. The God of Small Things
20. India
21. Premchand
22. Lexicographer
23. Bibliophile
24. Ratnakar
25. Vikram Seth
26. Bankim Chandra Chatterji
27. Pali
28. R.K. Narayan
29. Anand Math
30. Dr. Rajendra Prasad
31. London and Paris
32. Premchand
33. Amrita Pritam
34. Urdu and Persian
35. A Suitable Boy
36. 18
37. Midnight's Children
38. John Milton
39. Geoffrey Chaucer
40. Boris Pasternak

ART & CULTURE

1. Leonardo da Vinci
2. Bihu
3. Flute
4. Italy
5. Gujarat
6. Ballerina
7. Haryana
8. Onam
9. Veena
10. Kimono
11. Kathakali
12. Violin
13. Sarod
14. Maharashtra
15. Santoor
16. Kuchipudi
17. Kathak
18. Brazil
19. Louvre (Paris)
20. Baton

ANSWERS

RELIGION & MYTHOLOGY

1. Guru Nanak
2. Lumbini (Nepal)
3. Mecca (Saudi Arabia)
4. Ramayana
5. Konark (Orissa)
6. Qur'an
7. Christianity
8. Islam
9. Guru Ram Das
10. Jesus Christ
11. Lord Shiva
12. Talwandi (now Nankana Saheb, Pakistan)
13. John
14. Kumbh Fair
15. Hajj
16. Lama
17. Lord Ganesha
18. Lakshmi
19. 18 days
20. Bhagirath
21. Japan
22. Ramadan
23. Bethlehem
24. Song of the Lord
25. Guru Ram Das
26. Bodh Gaya (Bihar)
27. Srirangam Temple (Tiruchirappalli, Tamil Nadu)
28. Se Cathedral (Old Goa)
29. Basilica of St. Peter (Vatican City)
30. Shah Faisal Mosque (Pakistan)
31. Pahalgam (Kashmir)
32. Tirupati Temple (Andhra Pradesh)
33. Bheema
34. Akbar
35. Divine Faith
36. Lord Shiva
37. Jerusalem
38. Vibhishana
39. St. Thomas
40. Friday
41. Mecca (Saudi Arabia)
42. Puri (Orissa)
43. Parsees
44. Lord Ganesha
45. Disciple
46. Submission
47. Jainism
48. Islam
49. Bahai
50. Duhshala
51. Guru Arjun Dev
52. Guru Arjun Dev
53. Rig Veda
54. Lord Vishnu
55. Cambodia
56. Sugreeva
57. Parsees
58. Valmiki
59. Khwaja Muin-ud-din Chishti
60. Lord Jagannath

MONUMENTS & OTHER STRUCTURES

1. Statue of Liberty
2. Paris
3. Buland Darwaza (Fatehpur Sikri)
4. Qutub Minar
5. Chandigarh
6. Ustaad Isa
7. Rashtrapati Bhavan
8. Delhi Gate
9. Kharagpur Railway Platform (West Bengal)
10. Petronas Twin Towers
11. Shreepati Arcade (Mumbai)
12. Sir Edward Baker
13. Buckingham Palace
14. New Delhi
15. Four
16. Delhi
17. Statue of Lord Hanumana (Nandura, Maharashtra)
18. Bhakra Nangal Dam (Punjab)
19. Pentagon
20. Victoria Memorial (Kolkata)
21. CN Tower (Toronto)
22. Pentagon
23. Tihar Central Jail (New Delhi)
24. Alexandre Gustave Eiffel
25. Rome (Italy)
26. France
27. 72.5 m
28. Nek Chand
29. India Gate
30. Hyderabad
31. Kuala Lumpur (Malaysia)
32. Chittor (Rajasthan)
33. Howrah Bridge
34. Akashi Kaikyo Bridge (Japan)
35. Delhi
36. George Washington, Thomas Jefferson, Theodore Roosevelt and Abraham Lincoln
37. King Khalid International Airport (Saudi Arabia)
38. Kolkata
39. India Gate
40. Iltutmish

MISCELLANEOUS

1. China
2. Maharaja
3. Progress
4. India
5. Pragati Maidan (New Delhi)
6. Vande Mataram
7. The President of India
8. Shatabdi Express
9. September 5
10. The punishment of death
11. USA
12. National Library (Kolkata)
13. Library of Congress (Washington, DC)
14. 500
15. Philately
16. Mint
17. PARAM
18. Mughal Garden
19. 52 seconds
20. State Bank of India (SBI)
21. UK
22. GT Road (2,400 km)
23. New Delhi
24. The President of India
25. Hardness
26. 24
27. Value Payable Post
28. Ganga and Yamuna
29. Reserve Bank of India (RBI)
30. Crescent
31. Li (China)
32. 29
33. National mourning
34. Glass bangles
35. Pokhran (Rajasthan)
36. Modem
37. Xerox machine
38. 35 years
39. Big Ben
40. Zero
41. Bengal Gazette
42. Dharavi (Mumbai)
43. TGV Express (France)
44. Watches
45. International Standard Book Number
46. Mumbai
47. Italy
48. Courage & Sacrifice
49. Truth & Peace
50. Faith & Prosperity
51. Mexico City
52. Dessert
53. A female dog (named Laika)
54. The President's Bodyguard
55. Teller
56. 1985
57. Mysore (Karnataka)
58. Bharat Ratna
59. Param Vir Chakra
60. India
61. India
62. Oxford University
63. Chennai
64. Nobel Prize
65. IBM
66. Nathuram Godse
67. Hangar
68. The Times of India
69. Sher Shah Suri
70. USA
71. Pakistan
72. Inter-Services Intelligence
73. Geneva (Switzerland)
74. Butcher
75. Satyameva Jayate
76. Japan
77. USA
78. Uttar Pradesh
79. World Bank
80. Siachen
81. Sweden
82. Six
83. KLM (Netherlands)
84. India
85. USA
86. New York
87. Khadi
88. Nine

ANSWERS

89. Moradabad
90. All India Institute of Medical Sciences
91. Uncle Sam
92. Brazil
93. Custom Duty
94. Four
95. Sep. 11, 2001
96. 25 years
97. Diet
98. West Bengal
99. Science
100. Fields Medal
101. Maple leaf
102. Persian (Farsi)
103. Hero Cycles Ltd. (India)
104. Germany
105. Demography
106. December 10
107. USA
108. Indira Gandhi National Open University
109. Sherwood Forest
110. New Zealand
111. China (14 countries)
112. Germany
113. 2 : 3
114. Summons
115. Yes
116. USA
117. Question Hour
118. Arsenal
119. Deccan Queen
120. Jammu Tawi to Kanyakumari
121. Dalal Street
122. December 1
123. Liberation Tigers of Tamil Eelam
124. Prayagraj Express (New Delhi–Allahabad, 24 boggies)
125. Economics
126. Portuguese
127. 2.54 cm
128. 1.6 km
129. 454 g
130. 4.55 litres
131. Patwari
132. Australia
133. Vatican City
134. Bangalore
135. Dehradun
136. Khadakwasla (Maharashtra)
137. Union Carbide
138. Vice-President of India
139. Journalism
140. The Hague (Netherlands)
141. Air Force-One
142. Philippines
143. Lyon (France)
144. Downing Street
145. October 24
146. South Asian Association for Regional Corporation
147. Comprehensive Test Ban Treaty
148. Agriculture
149. Russia
150. Red Cross
151. The President of India
152. 1989
153. Newspapers & Journalists
154. Intel Corporation
155. June 5
156. The Wall Street
157. Franklin D. Roosevelt
158. Methyl isocyanate
159. 1974
160. Article 352

PICTURE QUIZ

1. Shyam Benegal
2. Madhubala
3. Marilyn Monroe
4. Dalai Lama
5. Nelson Mandela
6. V.S. Naipaul
7. Rakesh Sharma
8. Gary Kasparov
9. Leander Paes

ILLUSTRATIONS

Page Name/Description

1. Titanic, sank in the North Atlantic; April 1912; about 1,500 people were drowned.

4. Elephant
Giant panda
Kangaroo
Lion

5. Chimpanzee (An ape)
Tiger
Octopus
Bison

6. Platypus
Spoonbill
Bald eagle
Pelican

7. Polar bear
Harpy eagle
Crane
Orang-utan

8. Sloth
Moose (also known as Elk)
Andean condor
Capybara

9. Leaves
Mushroom
Redwood trees

10. The medical rating for perfect vision is 6/6 (metres).

12. Iris is responsible for the colour of the eyes.

13. Volcanoes
Electric bulb
Yuri Gagarin
Neil Armstrong

14. Spider, the cause of arachnophobia
Carbon monoxide present in the automobile exhaust can cause cancer.

15. Alfred Bernhard Nobel
Ship

16. Michael Faraday
Thomas Alva Edison

17. Galileo Galilei

18. Albert Einstein
Hovercraft
The milk contains lactic acid.

19. A veterinarian
Dr. Har Gobind Khorana

20. Baseball is the national game of USA.
Pele

21. Polo
Dhyan Chand
Vishwanathan Anand

22. P.T. Usha
Sachin Tendulkar

23. Sir Don Bradman

24. Cassius Clay (Muhammad Ali)

25. Adolf Hitler
Akbar
Greek civilization

26. Kshatrapati Shivaji
Attack on Pearl Harbour

27. Egyptian kings were called Pharaohs.
Sardar Vallabhbhai Patel
American War of Independence

36. Satyajit Ray
Dilip Kumar
Amitabh Bachchan
Lata Mangeshkar

37. Dr. Rajendra Prasad
Dr. S. Radhakrishnan
Charlie Chaplin
George Washington

38. Abraham Lincoln
Rabindranath Tagore
Sarojini Naidu
Rajiv Gandhi

39. Salim Ali
Dr. Zakir Husain
Lal Bahadur Shastri
Lala Lajpat Rai

40. Neelam Sanjiva Reddy
Mother Teresa
Dr. Amartya Sen

41. Charan Singh
William Shakespeare
Fakhruddin Ali Ahmad

42. Premchand

43. A bibliophile
Mirza Ghalib

44. Violin
A Japanese woman wearing kimono
A music conductor carrying a baton

45. Guru Nanak
Jesus Christ
Lakshmi

46. Lord Buddha
Lord Shiva

47. Lord Ganesha
Lord Vishnu

48. Statue of Liberty

49. Mount Rushmore

50. Celebrating Teachers' Day

52. TGV Express

55. Bicycle